+234express®

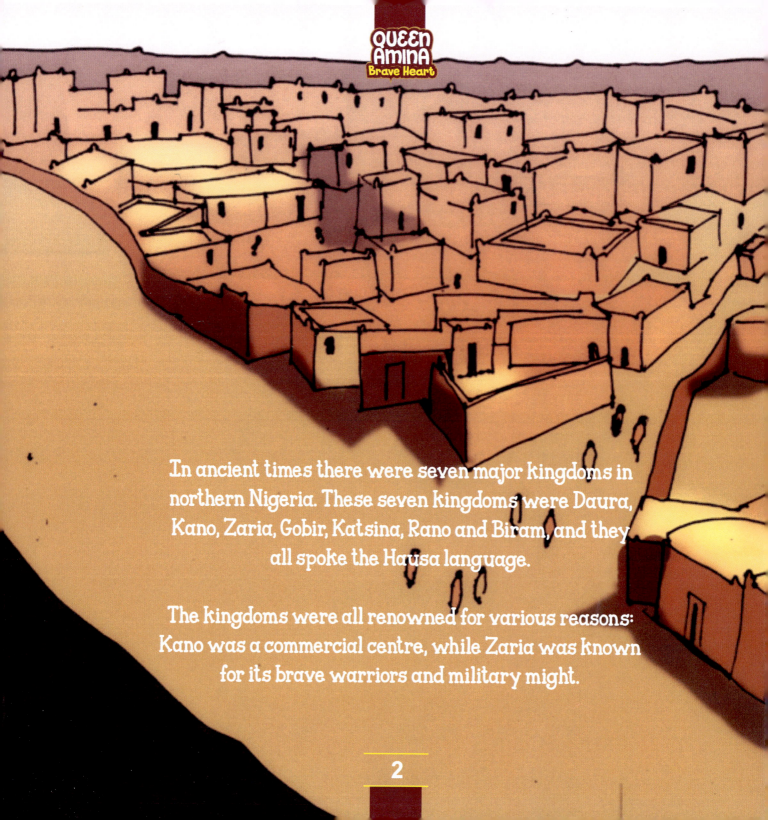

In ancient times there were seven major kingdoms in northern Nigeria. These seven kingdoms were Daura, Kano, Zaria, Gobir, Katsina, Rano and Biram, and they all spoke the Hausa language.

The kingdoms were all renowned for various reasons: Kano was a commercial centre, while Zaria was known for its brave warriors and military might.

Zaria's brave warriors and Calvary helped to protect the city and the other kingdoms from attacks by enemies and slave raiders.

QUEEN AMINA
Brave Heart

In the year 1533, a baby girl is born into the royal house of Bakwa in Zaria. She is named Amina by her parents.

Her parents were of the ruling class and were wealthy merchants who traded in leather goods, cloth, kola nuts, salt, horses, and metals.

Amina's naming ceremony attracts a huge crowd to the palace in Zaria. Friends and family members bring many gifts as they celebrate.

Growing up among her peers in the ancient Zaria city, Amina was like every other child enjoying the peace and prosperity that the kingdom witnessed under the reign of King Bakwa, but a great future lay ahead of her.

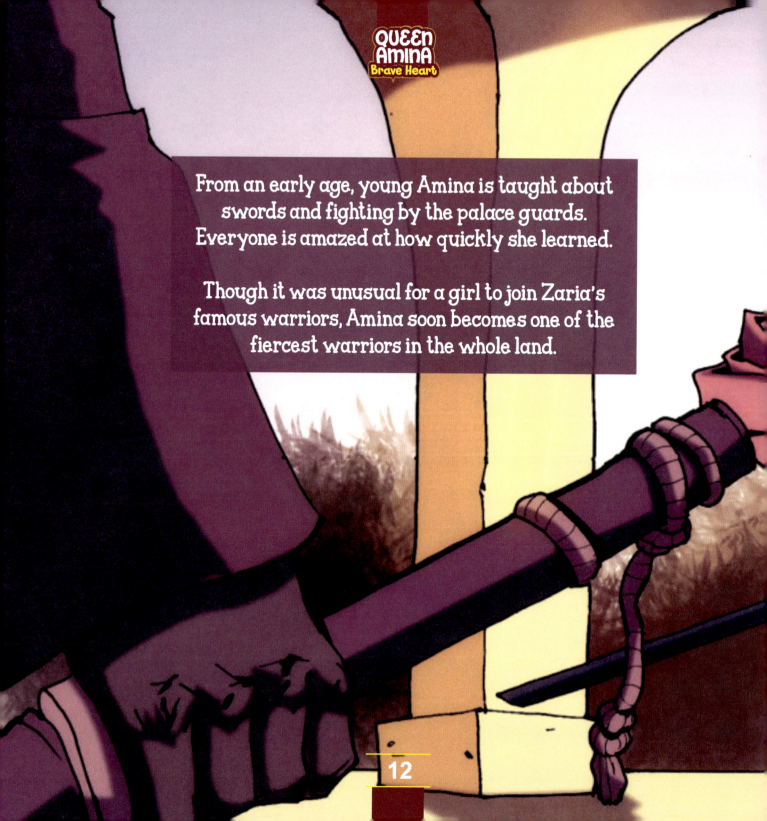

From an early age, young Amina is taught about swords and fighting by the palace guards. Everyone is amazed at how quickly she learned.

Though it was unusual for a girl to join Zaria's famous warriors, Amina soon becomes one of the fiercest warriors in the whole land.

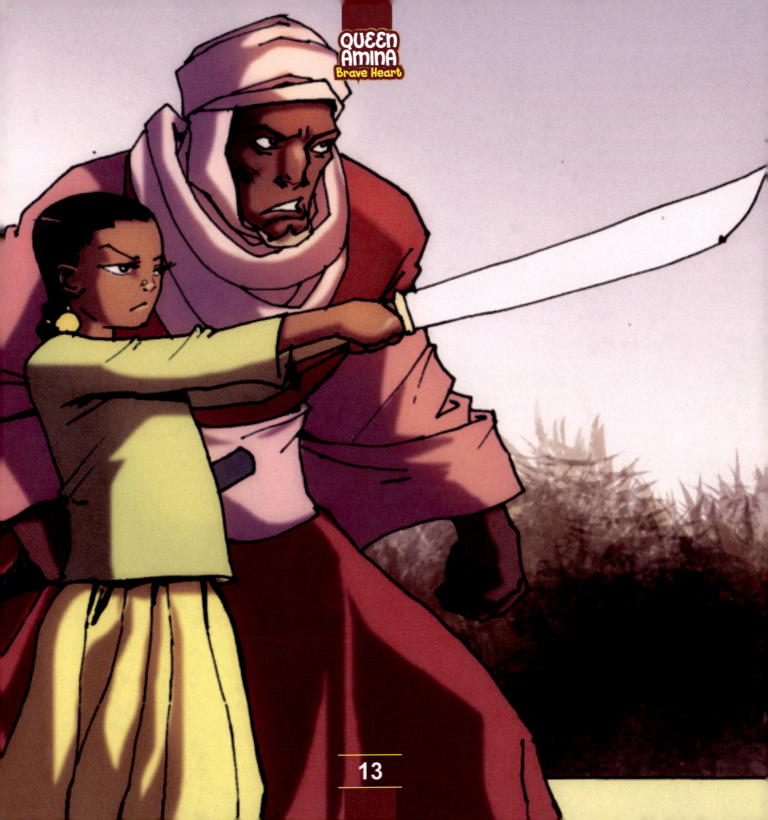

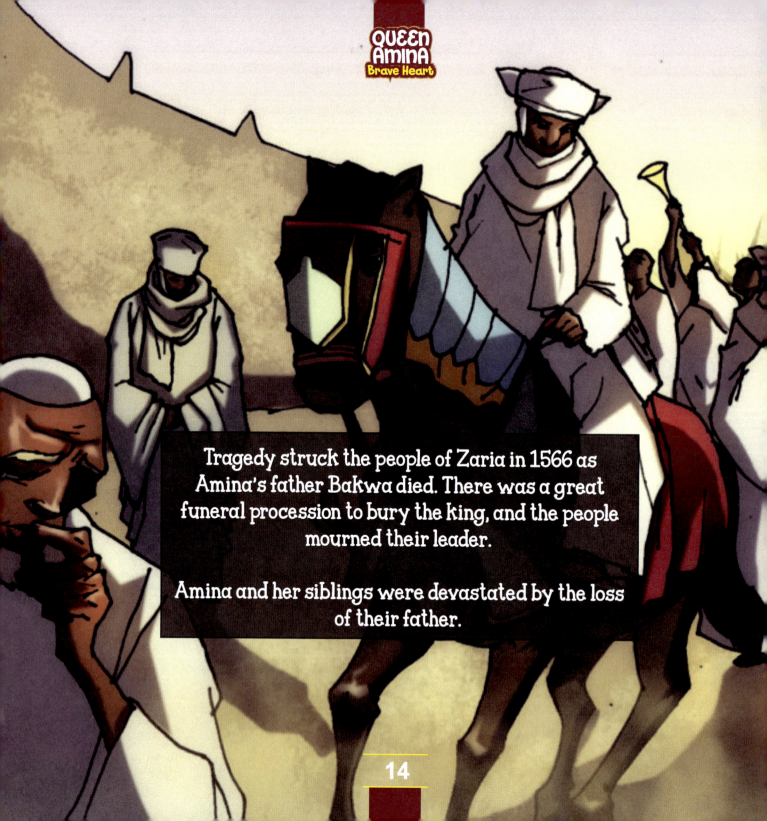

Tragedy struck the people of Zaria in 1566 as Amina's father Bakwa died. There was a great funeral procession to bury the king, and the people mourned their leader.

Amina and her siblings were devastated by the loss of their father.

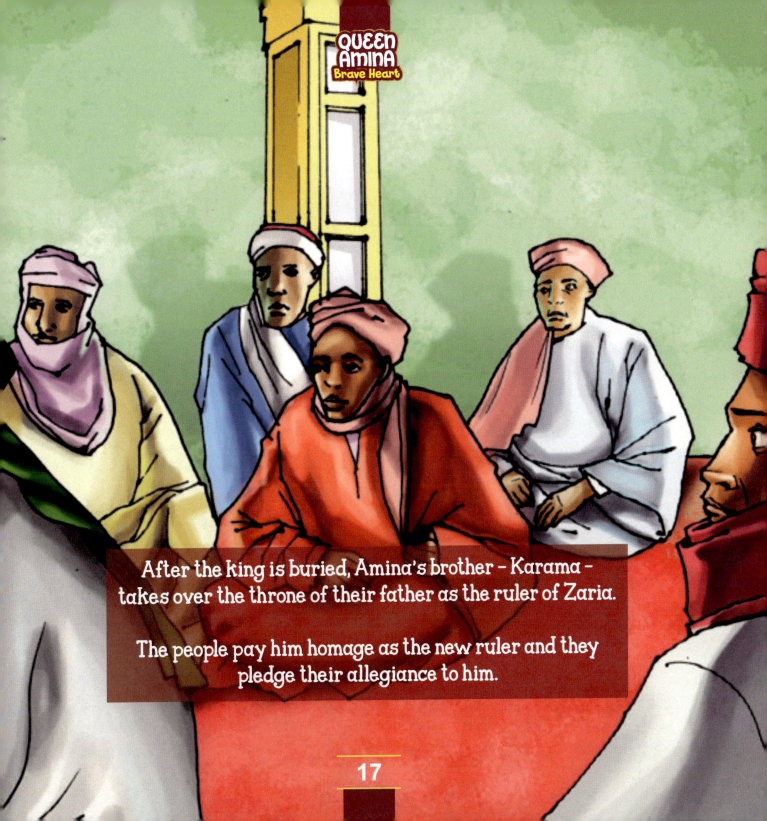

After the king is buried, Amina's brother – Karama – takes over the throne of their father as the ruler of Zaria.

The people pay him homage as the new ruler and they pledge their allegiance to him.

The new king Karama continues in the ways of his father before him. He protects the people from invaders and ensures there is peace in the land. He encourages everyone to work hard and earn a decent living.

While her brother ruled over the affairs of the kingdom, Amina was appointed as the head of Zaria's cavalry. As a brave and skilled warrior, she inspires the army to greater heights and they achieve many victories against the kingdom's enemies.

Tales of Amina's skills and courage soon travel far and wide and she is revered in all the Hausa kingdoms and beyond.

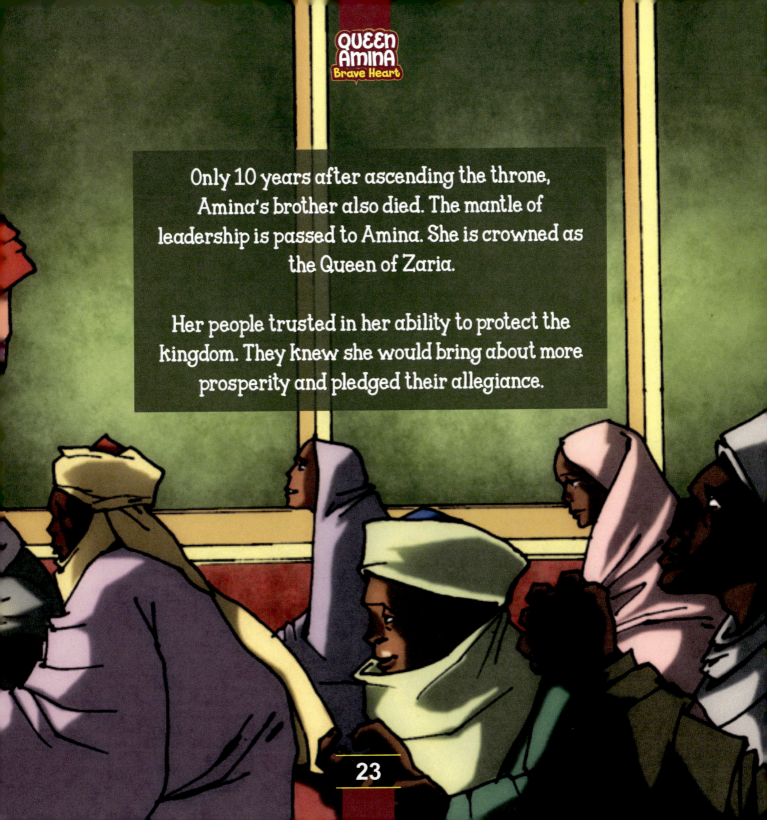

Only 10 years after ascending the throne, Amina's brother also died. The mantle of leadership is passed to Amina. She is crowned as the Queen of Zaria.

Her people trusted in her ability to protect the kingdom. They knew she would bring about more prosperity and pledged their allegiance.

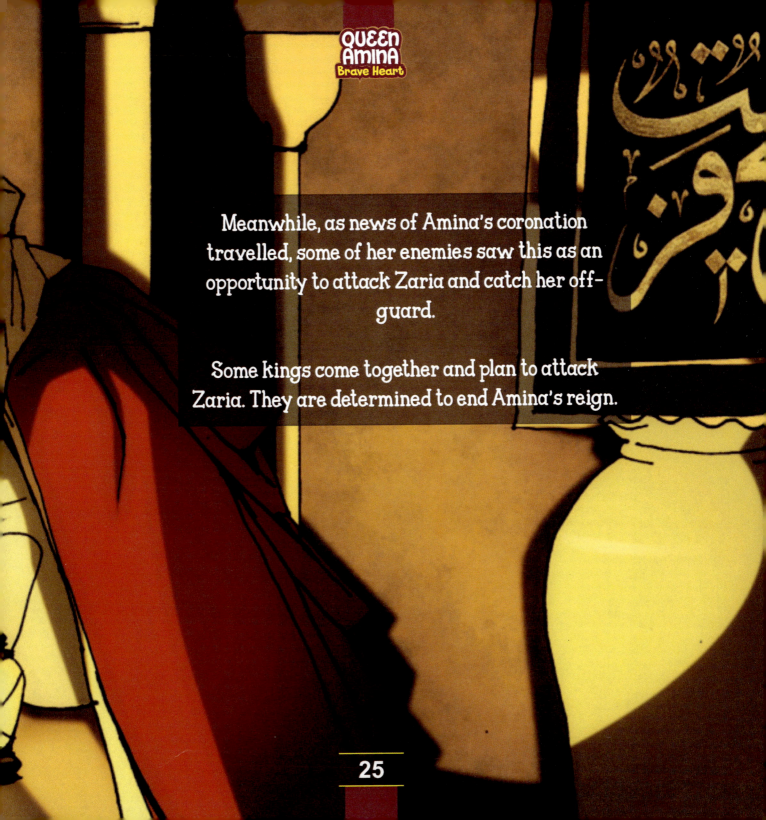

Meanwhile, as news of Amina's coronation travelled, some of her enemies saw this as an opportunity to attack Zaria and catch her off-guard.

Some kings come together and plan to attack Zaria. They are determined to end Amina's reign.

Though Queen Amina is made aware that some of her enemies were keen on attacking Zaria, she encourages the people to go about their daily routines without fear.

She trusted in the abilities of her army to defend the city from all invaders.

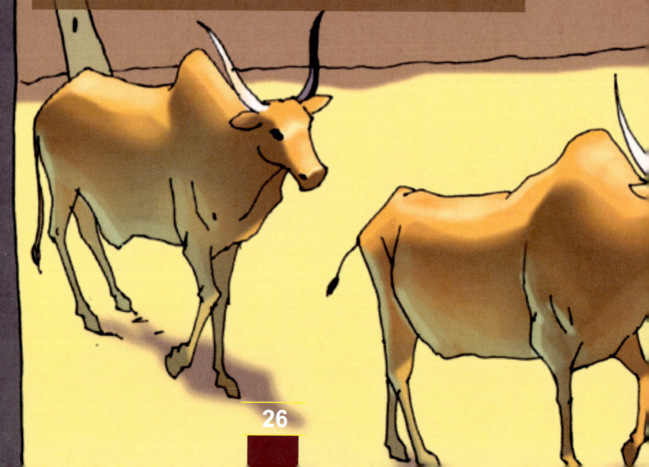

To further protect the people of Zaria, Queen Amina builds tall protective walls around the city.

The people of Zaria felt safe, and they prospered in various businesses; trading gold, precious metals and crops with merchants from far and wide.

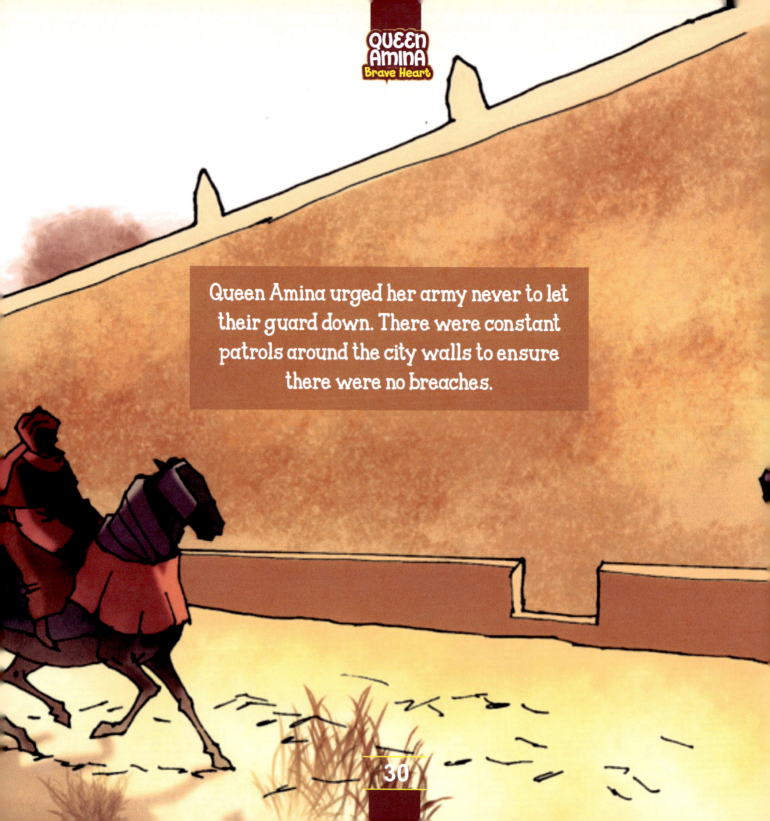

Queen Amina urged her army never to let their guard down. There were constant patrols around the city walls to ensure there were no breaches.

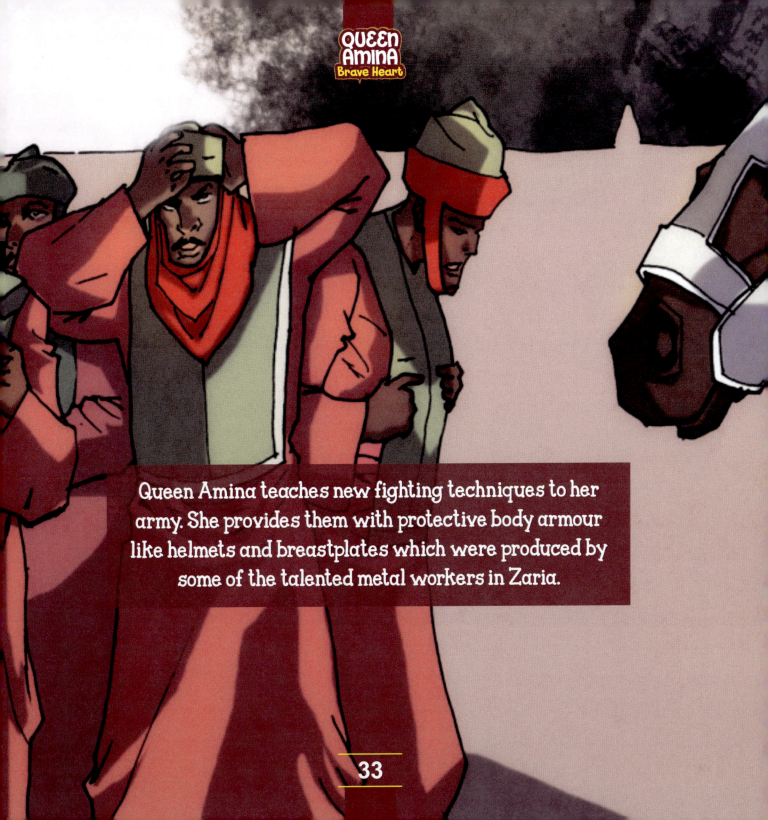

Queen Amina teaches new fighting techniques to her army. She provides them with protective body armour like helmets and breastplates which were produced by some of the talented metal workers in Zaria.

With their plans complete, and their armies gathered, Queen Amina's enemies begin their invasion march to Zaria.

They camp in large numbers some distance from Zaria; waiting for the perfect opportunity to strike.

The invading armies laid siege to some of the trade routes leading into Zaria and rob traders on their way back to the city. Some merchants are attacked and even killed by the invading armies and their goods were seized by the soldiers.

As soon as Queen Amina gets news of approaching armies, she assembles her army and leads them out of the city to repel the invaders. The soldiers are well-equipped and well-trained. They are ready for battle.

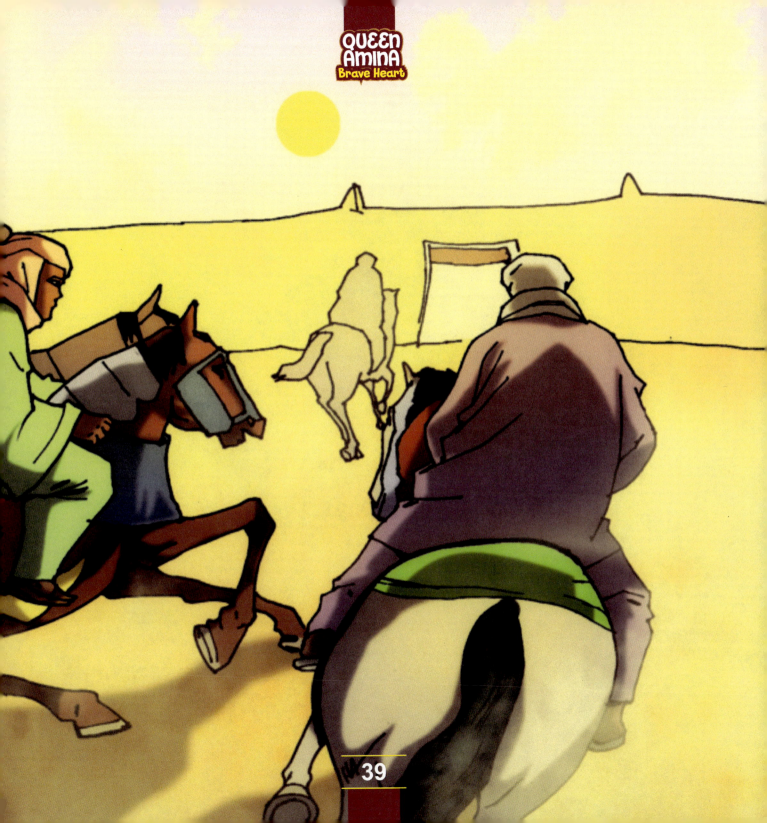

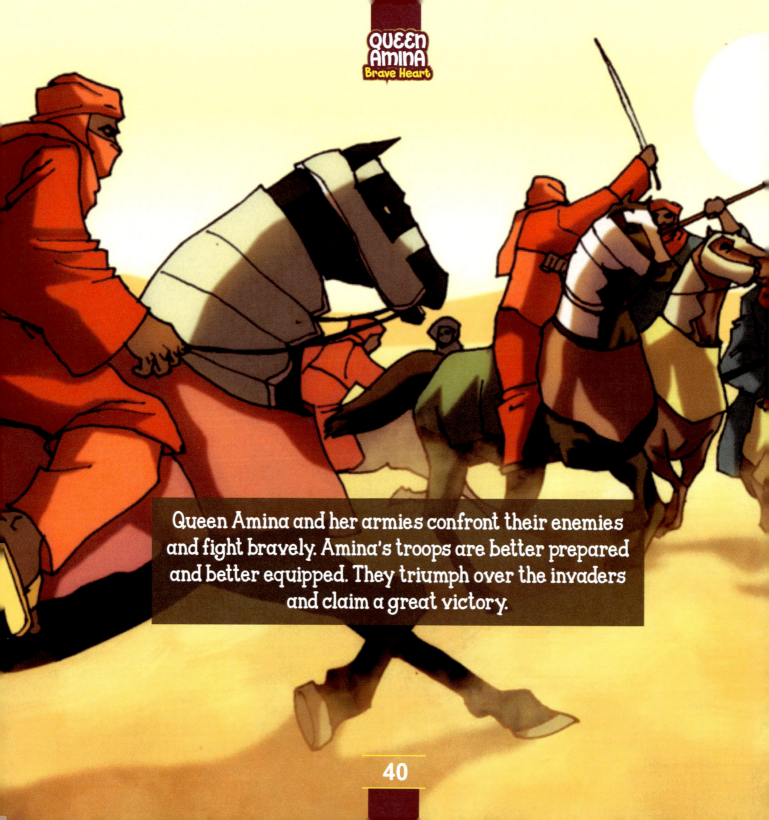

Queen Amina and her armies confront their enemies and fight bravely. Amina's troops are better prepared and better equipped. They triumph over the invaders and claim a great victory.

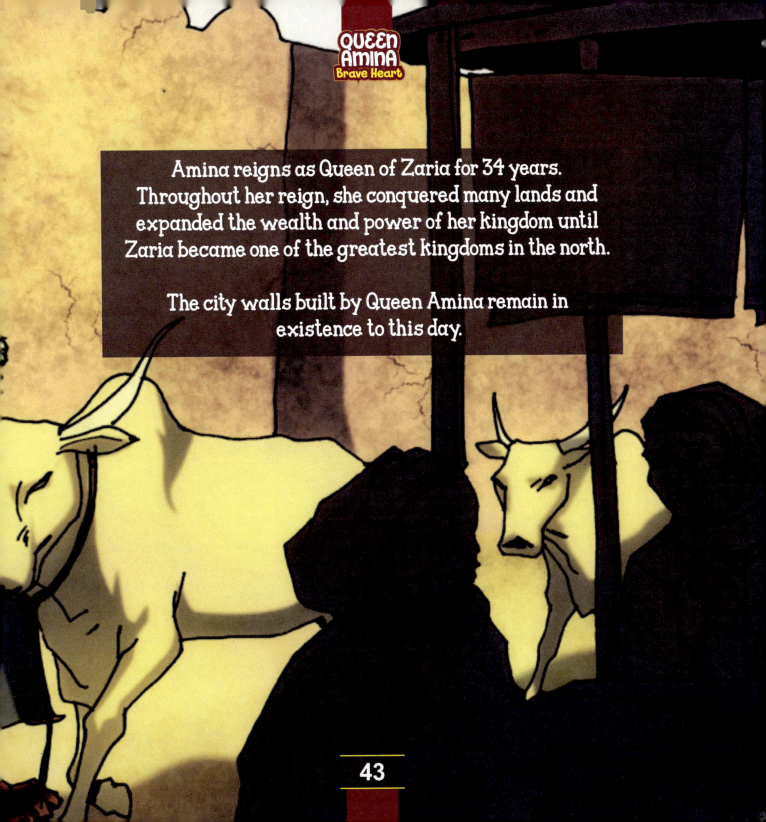

Amina reigns as Queen of Zaria for 34 years. Throughout her reign, she conquered many lands and expanded the wealth and power of her kingdom until Zaria became one of the greatest kingdoms in the north.

The city walls built by Queen Amina remain in existence to this day.

Made in the USA
Middletown, DE
26 July 2021